My Little
Word
Books

HAMPTON-BROWN

Contents

 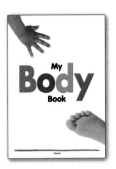
How to Assemble:

1. Tear one sheet off at perforation.
2. Fold on solid line.

 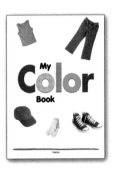

1. Tear two sheets off at perforation.
2. Fold both sheets together on solid line.
3. Staple along folded edge.
4. Cut interior pages only along dashed lines.

1. Tear two sheets off at perforation.
2. Fold both sheets together on solid line.
3. Staple along folded edge.

1. Tear one sheet off at perforation.
2. Cut out triangle at bottom along dashed lines.
3. Fold bottom of sheet on solid line, toward side that shows interior of home. This will allow folded sheet to stand up.

1. Tear three sheets off at perforation.
2. Fold all three sheets together on solid line.
3. Staple along folded edge.

How to Assemble:

6

1. Tear three sheets off at perforation.
2. Staple together at left edge.

7

 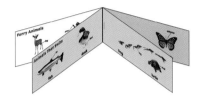

1. Tear two sheets off at perforation.
2. Cut each sheet in half along dashed line.
3. Stack resulting strips in this order, top to bottom: cover—bear/skunk—frog/turtle—bee/butterfly.
4. Staple together at left edge.

8

1. Tear two sheets off at perforation.
2. Fold both sheets together on solid line.
3. Staple along folded edge.
4. Cut **interior pages only** along dashed lines.

9

 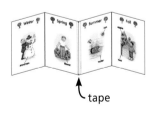

↳ tape

1. Tear one sheet off at perforation.
2. Cut in half along dashed line.
3. Fold each piece in half as shown.
4. Tape together to make accordion book.

10

1. Tear three sheets off at perforation.
2. Fold all three sheets together on solid line.
3. Staple along folded edge.

My Body Book

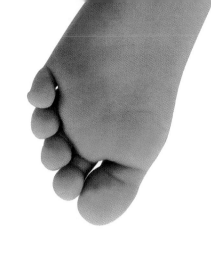

Name

My foot

Body

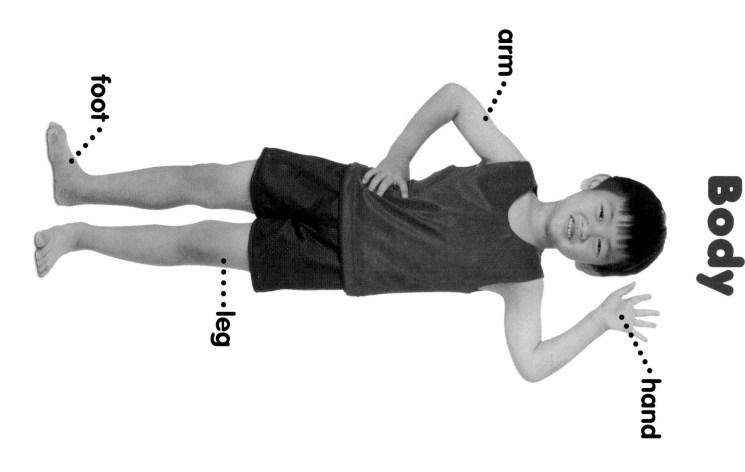

arm

foot

leg

hand

Face

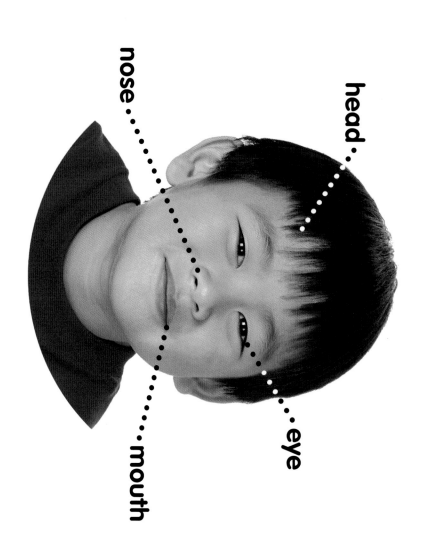

nose

head

eye

mouth

My Color Book

My **Color** Book

Name

My favorite color

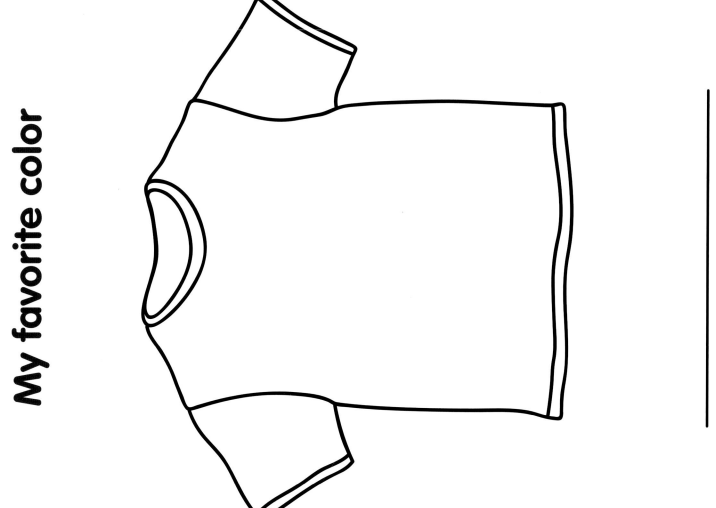

green

green

red

red

sock

shorts

T-shirt

coat

hat

boot

mitten

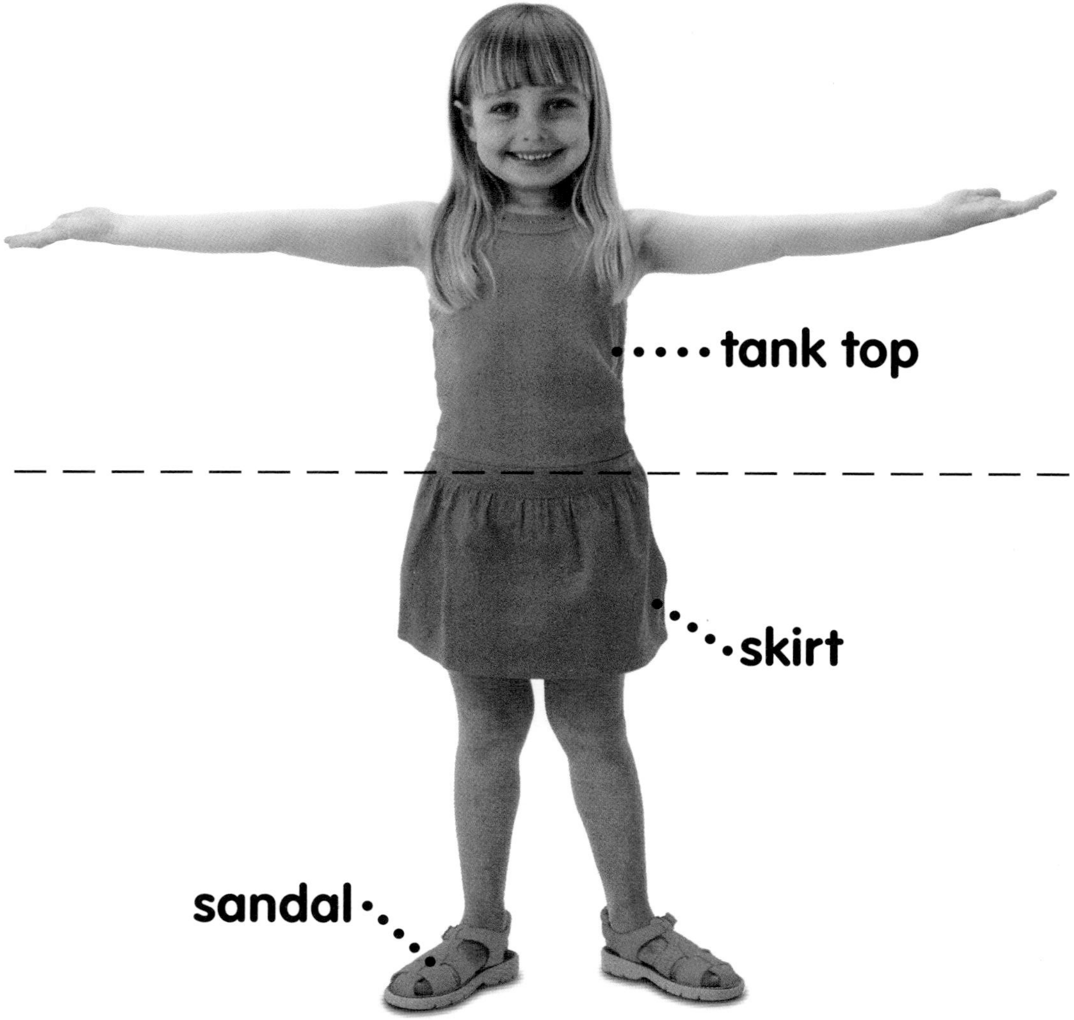

orange

tank top

skirt

sandal

blue

cap

jacket

jeans

glove

© Hampton-Brown

yellow

sneaker

shirt

pants

yellow

purple

shoe

dress

tights

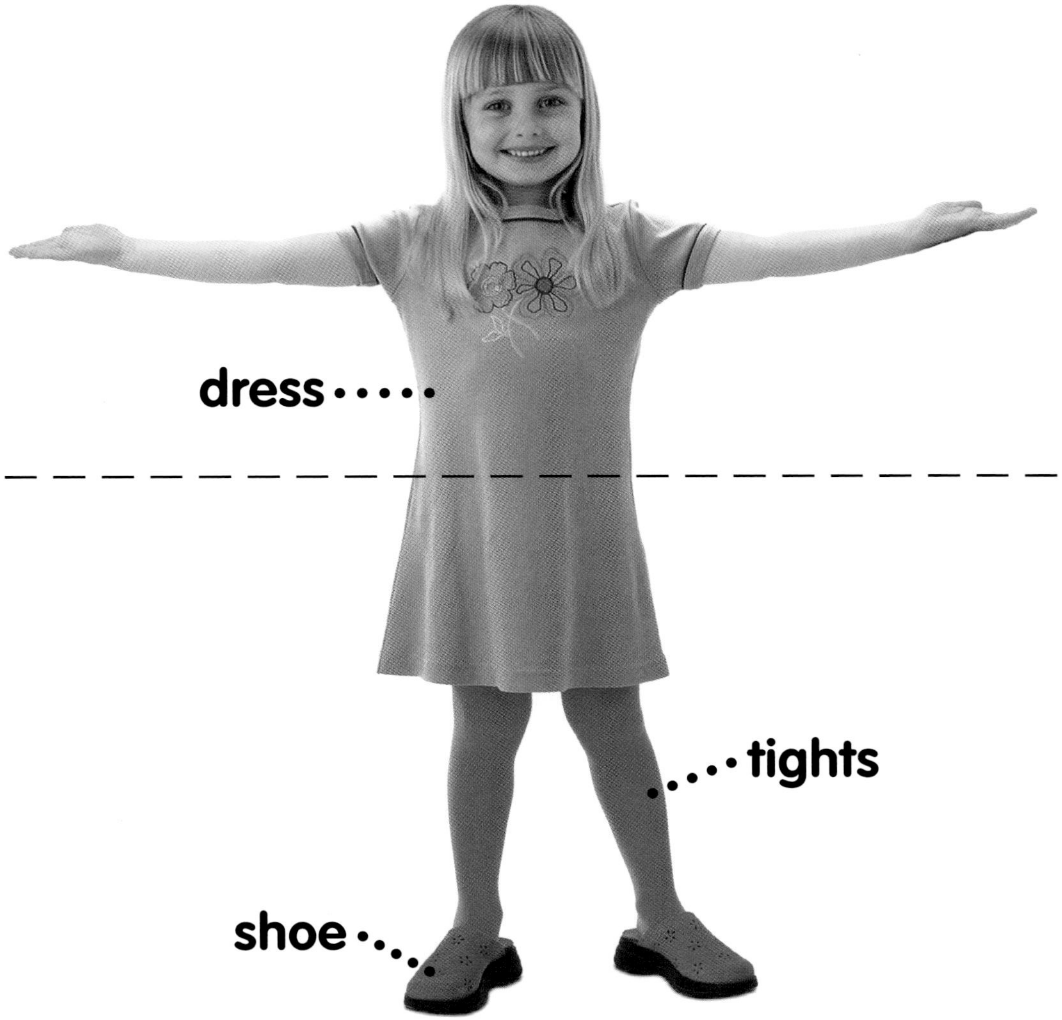

purple

My Food Book

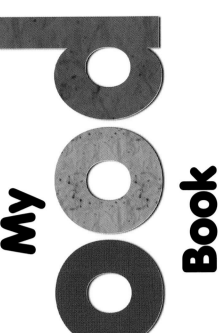

Name

Dessert

fresh fruit

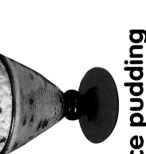

cookies

rice pudding

cake

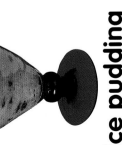

ice cream

watermelon

Breakfast

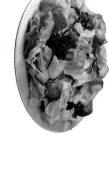
cereal

bread

bagel

banana

Vegetables

salad

broccoli

string beans

My dinner

Drinks

 milk

orange juice

water

Dinner

My breakfast

 beans

 salsa

 chicken and rice

 tortillas

Lunch

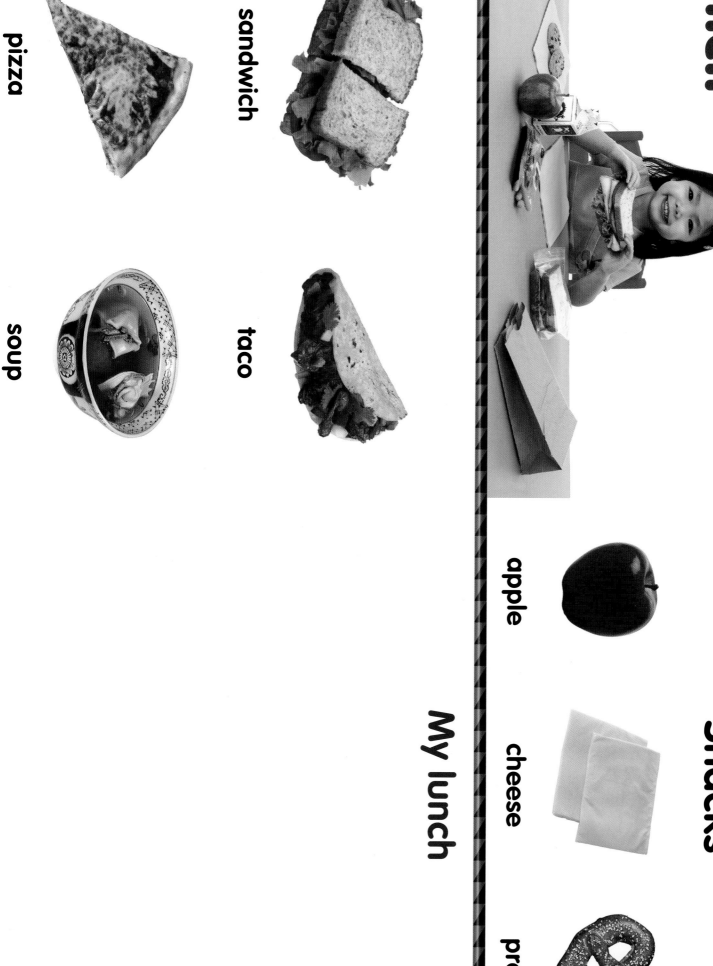

pizza

sandwich

soup

taco

Snacks

apple

cheese

pretzel

My lunch

My **Home**

Book

Name

In my home

lamp

table

sofa

bed

sink

rug

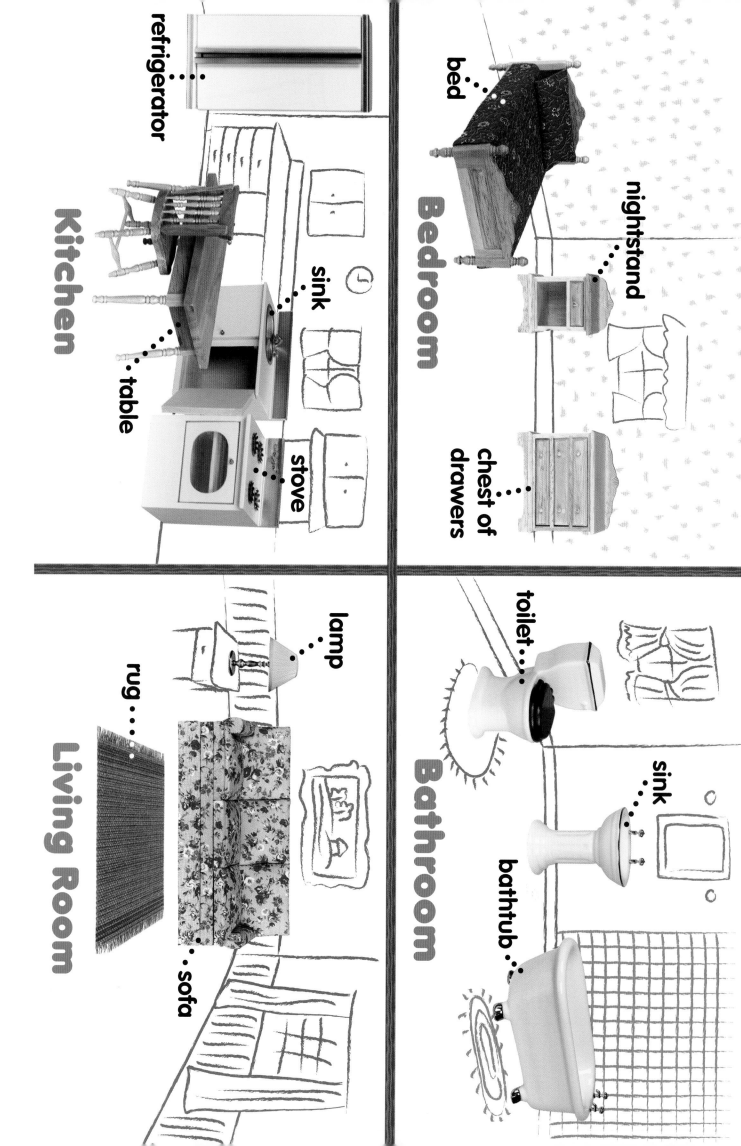

Bedroom

bed

nightstand

chest of drawers

Kitchen

refrigerator

sink

table

stove

Bathroom

toilet

sink

bathtub

Living Room

lamp

rug

sofa

My Family

Book

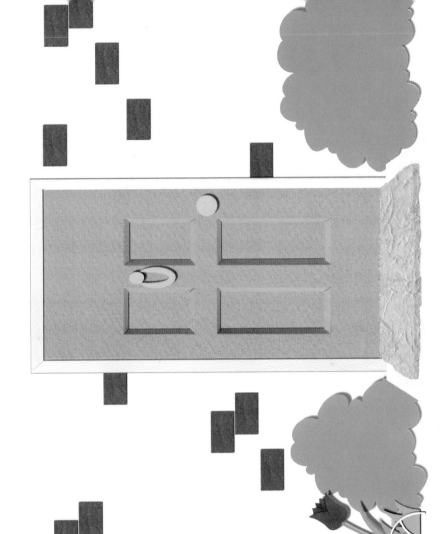

Name

My family

Knock, knock!
Who's there?

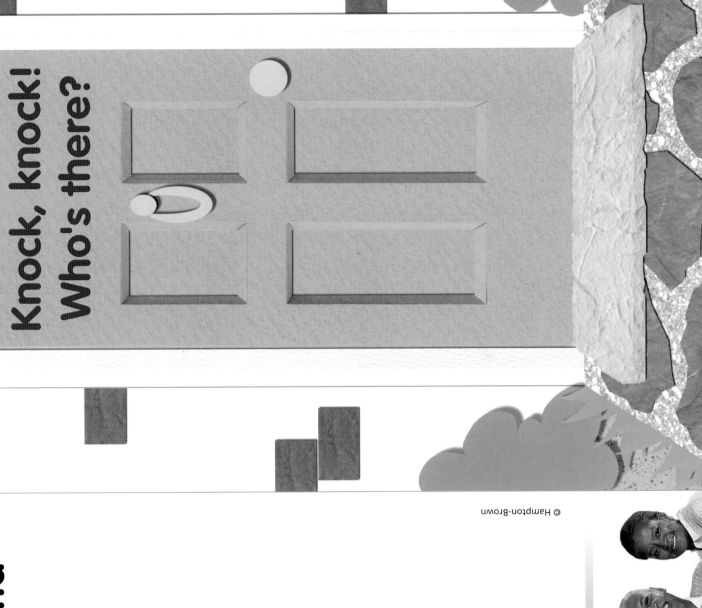

grandpa and grandma

mother and baby

Knock, knock!
Who's there?

Knock, knock! Who's there?

sister and brother

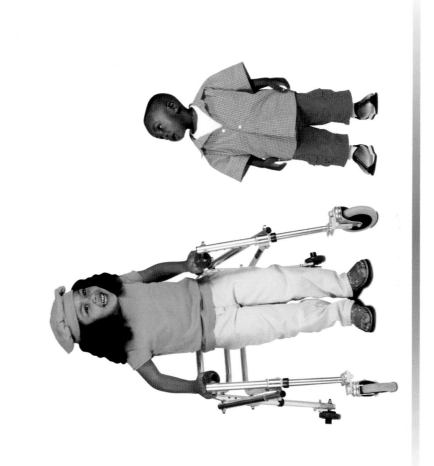

father

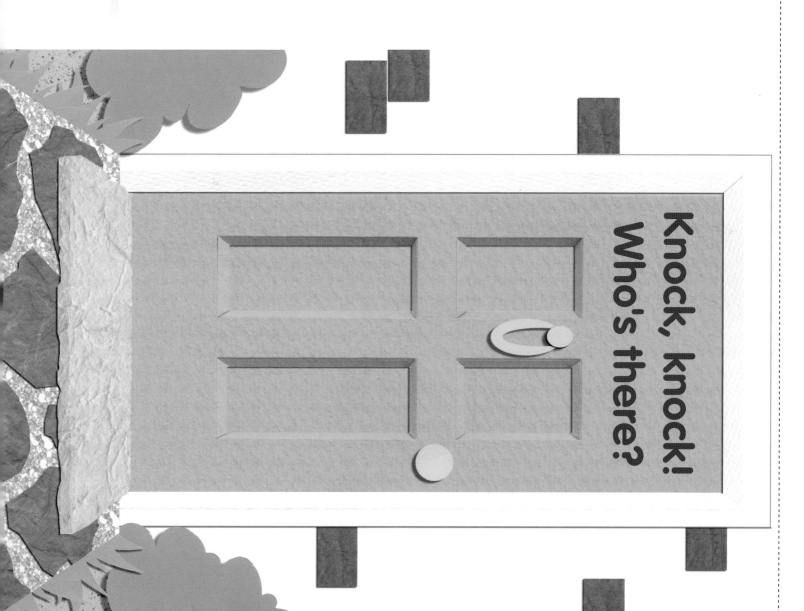

Knock, knock!
Who's there?

My Neighborhood Book

Name

fire truck

firefighter

mail truck

letter carrier

clerk

market

police officer

police car

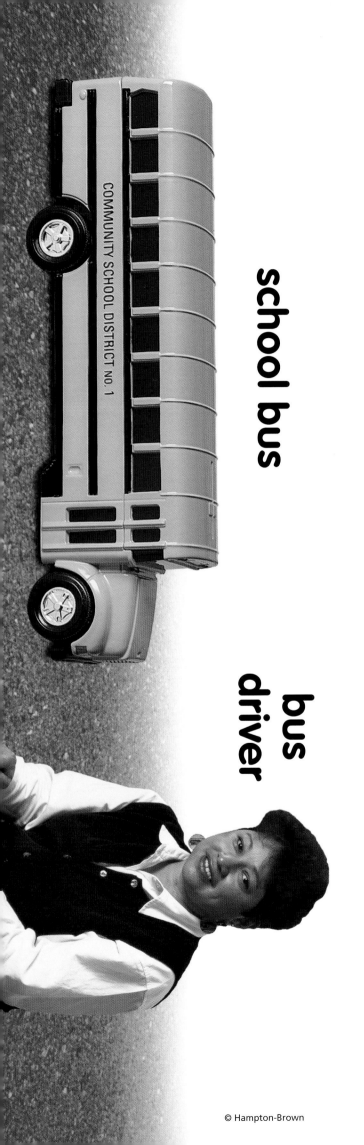

school bus

bus driver

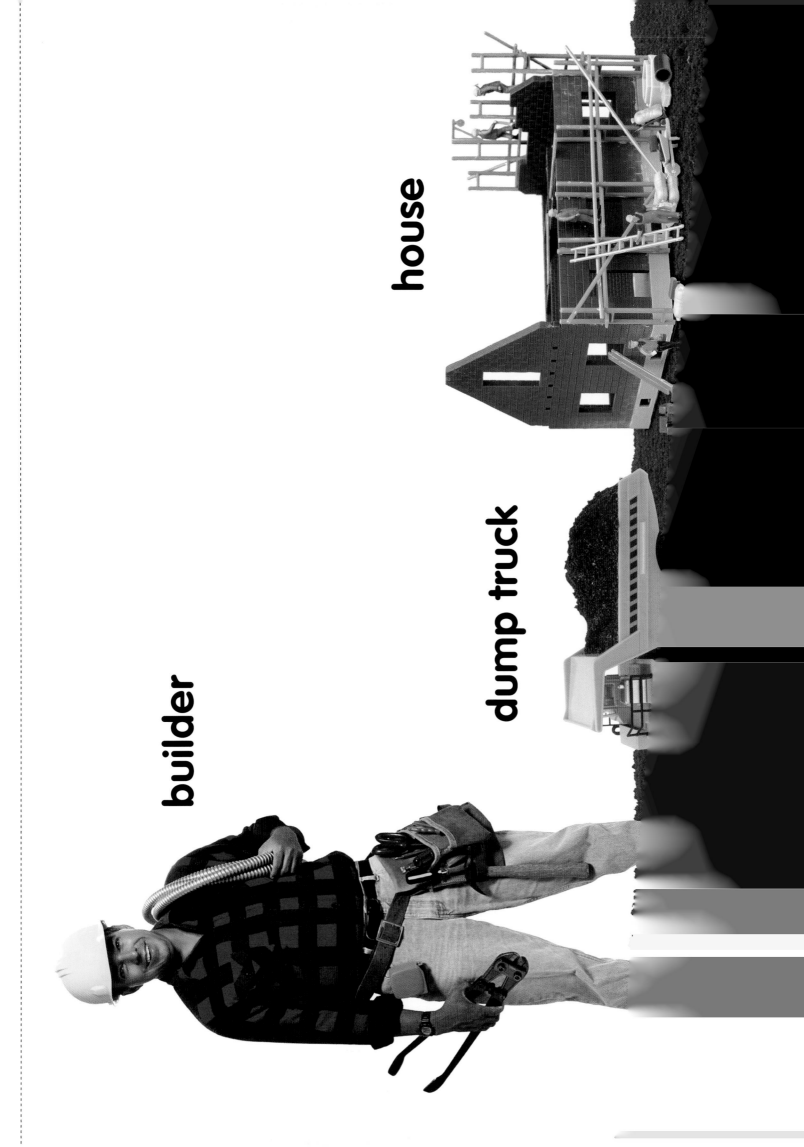

house

dump truck

builder

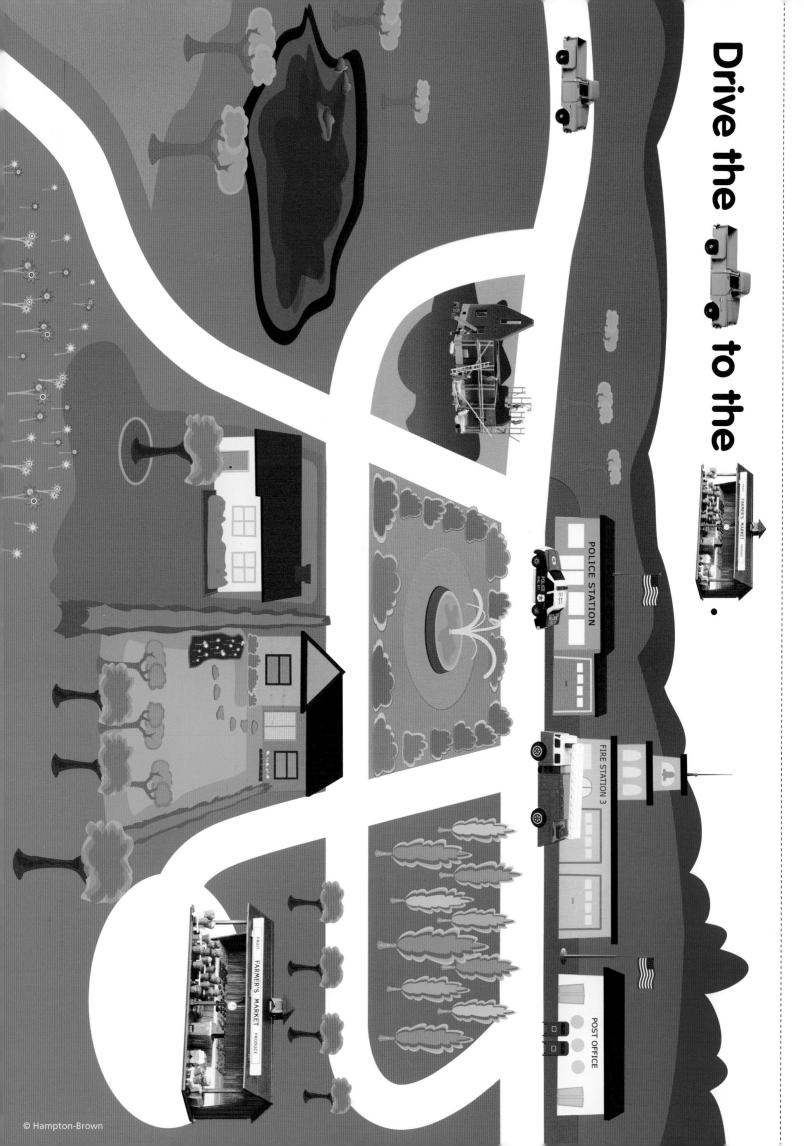

shell

turtle

leg

frog

My **Animal** Book

Name

Furry Animals

deer

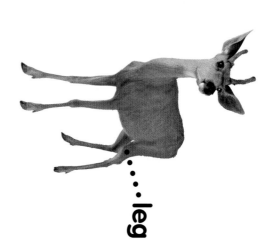

leg

raccoon

paw

Animals That Fly

eagle

wing

woodpecker

beak

tail

skunk

ear

bear

antenna

butterfly

eye

bee

Animals That Swim

fish

fin

duck

foot

Find 6 animals in the forest.

My Weather Book

Name _____

My favorite weather

snowy

snow

stormy

lightning

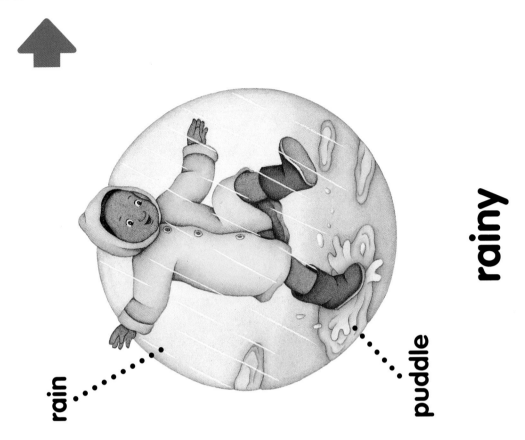

rainy

rain

puddle

windy

sunny

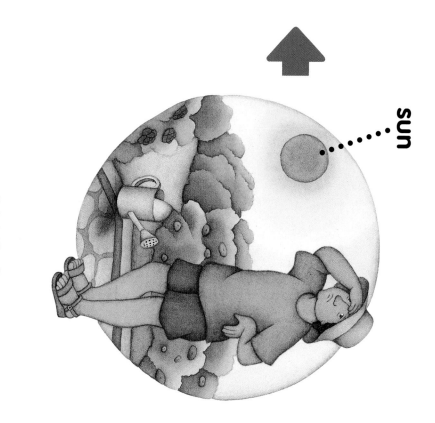

sun

cloudy

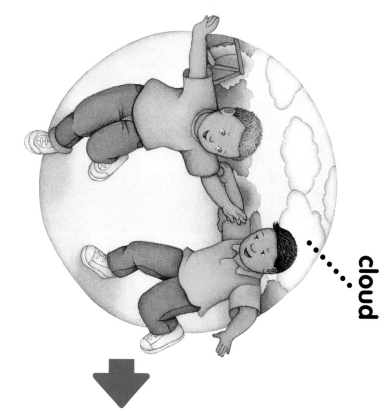

cloud

My Seasons Book

_____

Name

Match.

 # Winter

snowman

 # Spring

flower

 # Summer

sun

water

 # Fall

apple

tree

Color the plant.

green
yellow
red

My
Plant
Book

Name

1 seed

10 pods

seed ····· 🫘

Picking

9 ladybugs

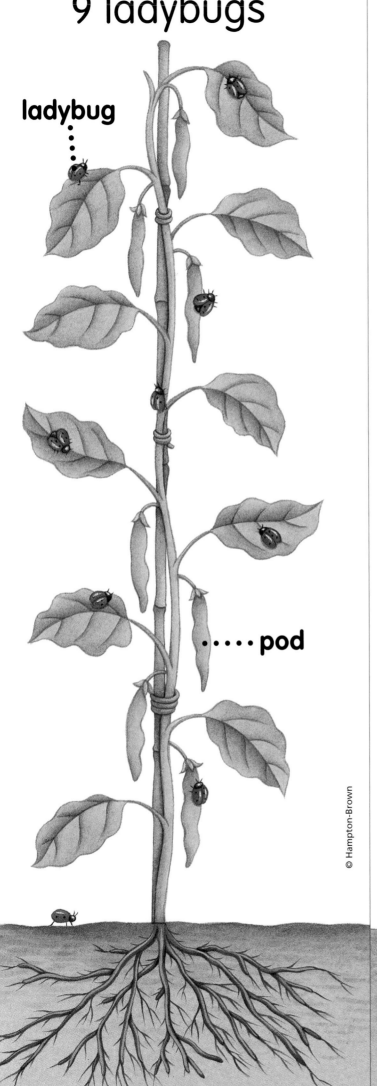

ladybug

pod

2 birds

bird

© Hampton-Brown

Planting

3 worms

8 butterflies

butterfly

leaf

root

worm

Digging

7 flowers

flower

4 bees

bee

Watering

5 leaves

6 weeds

bud · · · · ·

leaf

· · · · · stem

weed

Weeding